Until the Rain

Until the Rain

Conversations with Christian Palestinian Women

Anne Sörman

Foreword by Rosemary Radford Ruether

RESOURCE *Publications* • Eugene, Oregon

UNTIL THE RAIN
Conversations with Christian Palestinian Women

Resource Publications
An Imprint of Wipf and Stock Publishers
199 W. 8th Ave., Suite 3
Eugene, OR 97401

www.wipfandstock.com

ISBN 13: 978-1-4982-0700-3

Manufactured in the U.S.A.   04/29/2015

For my sisters and for all the women around the world who pursue the struggle for peace and justice in their daily lives.

For, while the tale of how we suffer, and how we are delighted, and how we may triumph is never new, it always must be heard. There isn't any other tale to tell, it's the only light we've got in all this darkness.

—James Baldwin, "Sonny's Blues"

Contents

Foreword

This small but compelling manuscript tells the story of Swedish journalist Anne Sörman's interviews with Palestinian women in the Bethlehem, Ramallah and Jerusalem areas of Palestine, their experiences of the Israeli occupation and the struggle for justice. Sörman reflects on the implications of these women's testimony for Biblical interpretation and Palestinian liberation theology.

Nadia, a resident of Bethlehem, is the base for Sörman's discussions. She is nurturing Palestinian children with cancer and the book closes with her experience of developing and being operated on for cancer herself, surrounded by supportive family and friends. For Nadia, the occupation is deeply oppressive. There is a need for healing of its effects on the Palestinian people. Nadia's sister, Natasha, is an Orthodox nun residing in a convent in Jerusalem. She lives with forty-six other nuns and her traditional ways form the foundation for a life of prayer by which she witnesses against the oppression of the Occupation. Sörman stays with Natasha in the convent several times during her visits to Jerusalem and experiences this way of life that continues, largely unchanged by modernity and Israeli control.

Jean Zaru, a Quaker leader who lives in Ramallah, is an articulate critic of the Occupation and what it means for Palestinians to be oppressed by it. Although surrounded by Israeli settlements on nearby hills, Palestinians have little opportunity to talk with Israelis on a day-to-day basis. Zaru reflects on the irony of Westerners exhorting Palestinians to "love their enemies" with little understanding of what it means to live under occupation. For Zaru, the "structures of dominance" include male domination of women, and Palestinian liberation must include liberation of Palestinian women as well.

Palestinians experience much random violence from Israelis, especially soldiers. Lucy Thalihei, a theologian who works to expound the Palestinian Kairos document, witnessed the death of her father when Israeli soldiers hit him on the head with a machine gun. Nidal experienced this violence in a particularly horrific manner. While she and her husband were on the way to the hospital to deliver her baby, they were stopped at the Nablus checkpoint and interrogated. Then when they were allowed to drive off, the soldiers shot at their car, killing her husband and forcing her to strip and lie naked. Finally allowed to go to the hospital, she gave birth to her baby girl in the elevator on the way to the delivery room. Nidal was deeply angered and was able to survive only when other Palestinian women who had suffered similar violence formed a support group for her.

Several of these women are academically trained and work with Palestinian liberation theologians to coordinate conferences and develop the Sabeel Palestinian theological center in Jerusalem. One of them, Marwa Nasser, comes from an active Lutheran community in Bethlehem and acquired a desire to be a minister when she realized that Lutheran women were being ordained in the West. Although women are allowed to study scripture and to preach, the Palestinian Lutheran church is yet unready to ordain them.

Sörman's stories are deeply moving and give a vivid sense of what life under occupation means for Palestinian women, especially those who can relate it to theological reflection and Biblical interpretation. Most deeply, the book reflects her many years of sharing in the lives of Palestinians, particularly women, and what the occupation means for those who experience it from day to day.

Rosemary Radford Ruether
Claremont School of Theology

Preface

The Second Book of Samuel in the Hebrew Bible tells of a woman named Rizpah whose sons are sacrificed in the power struggle between the houses of Saul and David.

> *Then Rizpah the daughter of Aiah took sackcloth, and spread it on a rock for herself, from the beginning of harvest until rain fell on them from the heavens; she did not allow the birds of the air to come on the bodies by day, or the wild animals by night.* (2 Sam 21:10)

Was Rizpah driven by the depths of despair? Or was she protesting in a woman's silent anger?

The same kind of quiet defiance is playing itself out in contemporary Palestine. Is it grief or resistance—or the foundation of a new theology?

Acknowledgments

I would like to express my deepest gratitude to all the women who shared so generously of their time, thoughts and hearts. They have been a constant source of inspiration.

Anne Sörman
Enskededalen, Sweden
January 1, 2015

1

A Crack for the Light to Come In

It was late autumn 2009 when Mitri Raheb leaned forward and
said: "I've been expecting you to come back and write about
Palestinian theology." I took his words as both an invitation and a
call to action. He sent me a list of names and I spent the following
winter formulating questions and sending e-mails.

I knew right off that I wanted to present Palestinian theology
through the voices of women, the daily reality of life in the Occupied Territories as opposed to written documents and the words
of clergy.

I returned to Palestine in summer 2011 for several hot and
exhausting weeks.

Some of the women I had hoped to see were too busy. Others were taken aback: "Did Mitri really give you my name? That's
strange." But many shared generously of their knowledge, time and
thoughts. One meeting and set of questions led to another.

They came from different backgrounds, circumstances,
educational backgrounds and religious affiliations. Jean Zaru is a
Quaker and Marwa Nasser is a Lutheran, while Lucy Thalihej and
Nadia Harb are Catholics. Yasmine Khoury is a member of the Syr-
ian Orthodox Church and Nora Carmi belongs to the Armenian
Apostolic Orthodox Church. Lucy and Marwa have degrees in

theology, and several of the others have university training as well. Jean (the only Palestinian Christian woman who leads a religious community) and Nora have long been involved in ecumenical efforts. Natasha Al Zoghbi is a nun and Nadia is a social worker.

I met most of the women for the first time that summer. Nadia and Natasha, who are sisters, have been my friends for more than twenty years.

I started off with a few fairly general questions. How can you maintain your faith in the Christian gospel of love in violent and unjust times? How can a Palestinian Christian relate to the biblical stories about God's chosen people? What is the foundation of contemporary Palestinian theology? Where is it heading?

Perhaps the main reason I decided to focus on women is that experience tells me that they are the pillars of daily life in Palestine. And they are the people among whom I feel most profoundly at home. Men's voices had been heard all the way to Sweden. Now I wanted to explore the interplay between political, human, and existential issues from the perspective of women. I was eager to find out whether Palestinian theology changes, whether new doors and rooms open, when women articulate it.

Contextual theology arose in tandem with Marxist theory when Latin American clergy and theologians of the 1960s and 1970s found it necessary to articulate a creed that was relevant to poor farmers and laborers. The theology stressed the radical nature of the gospel, the notion that Christian salvation also embraced the here and now, that Jesus was the champion and advocate of the outcasts and underprivileged. A fundamental critique of power and the Church was often combined with an emphasis on freedom from poverty and oppression as opposed to salvation from personal suffering. Liberation theology emerged as the official term for this perspective, the roots of which lay in the popular struggle of the Latin American people. Contextual theology has become the umbrella concept for the interrelated theologies and points of view that derive their power and essence from a particular set of circumstances: the destinies and worldviews of Palestinian farmers, second generation immigrants in the suburbs of Europe, indigenous peoples, LGBT persons, people with disabilities, children, etc.

An Anglican priest by the name of Naim Ateek, who began to formulate a Palestinian theology of liberation in the early 1980s, eventually founded the Sabeel Ecumenical Liberation Theology Centre in East Jerusalem. As a theologian and pastor, he thought it necessary to relate to the complex conflict with Israel and to define a particular Palestinian Christian perspective. Proceeding from questions of justice and biblical interpretation, he critiqued the concepts of land, border, and kingdom in the Hebrew Bible. His focus is on the New Testament and Christ, who preaches a Kingdom of God without borders, setting the stage for a radical understanding of ownership, as well as national and geopolitical rights.

Ateek's theology has clear pastoral themes, affecting his view of the Bible—how can a congregation living under military occupation find consolation in scriptural stories and prayers? Is the God who inhabits the Bible capable of acknowledging Palestinian suffering?

The second most prominent contemporary Palestinian theologian is German-educated Mitri Raheb of the Bethlehem Lutheran Church. In addition to preaching, he has published a number of books and articles. He founded the Diyar Consortium, an ecumenical community development project, in Bethlehem and has arranged a series of international theological conferences. As opposed to Ateek, Raheb speaks of contextual rather than liberation theology. His focus is on strengthening the Palestinian cultural and religious identity, seeking new paths beyond traditional Western theology. I see him as a pastor and teacher motivated by the desire to reclaim the entire Bible for Palestinian Christianity.

Fernando Segovia, Oberlin Graduate Professor of New Testament and Early Christianity at the Vanderbilt University Divinity School, participated in a Bethlehem conference during summer 2011. He linked Palestinian theology to four different kinds of theory and practice:

3

1) Liberation theology, with roots in Latin American materialistic criticism of the Bible

2) Postcolonial theory and critique

3) Studies of minorities, race and ethnicity

4) Cultural studies, or the encounter between the history of religion and culture

What strikes me about Palestinian theology is that it arises from its unique propinquity to biblical stories and places. Bethlehem, the site of the manger in which Jesus was born, is located in the occupied West Bank. He appeared to his disciples by the sea of Tiberia in what is now Israel. He visited Simon the Leper—as well as Martha, Mary and Lazarus—in the village of Bethany, now cut off from Jerusalem by the Wall.

This traumatized and militarized area is where Jesus wandered, preached the gospel, was crucified and resurrected to eternal life. Palestinian theology is a response to the experience of expulsion, which began in 1948 when almost one million refugees were created, followed by exile, oppression, abandonment, and occupation. It also stems from a narrative with roots both in the soil and in historical events that vibrate with profound political and human resonance. Like the narratives of many downtrodden and dispossessed peoples, it is sustained by powerful emotions, homesickness, the need for a future, and a quest for affirmation.

I spoke with women, expecting to encounter hope and courage, to witness the gospel at work in the milieu from which it originated. It didn't take long, however, for me to realize that I was off track. The walls were higher and human forbearance that much greater. Fear and oppression had left deeper scars than I was willing to see. There was a difference, if only in cadence or gesture, between word and meaning.

A crack appeared for the light to come in. And maybe that's the only thing I can pass on.

2

Under the Almond Tree

There must be thousands of shawls in Jerusalem: white, pink, silver, silk, tulle, spangled, fringed, sequined and ribboned. Women toss them over their shoulders or knit them tightly around their heads, hiding both their temples and their necks. Many women match their shawls with their make-up and clip them to their hair. I enter a shop on one of East Jerusalem's narrow streets and rummage through piles of shawls. They are sorted by color and type of material, and I finally settle on a silk one with long fringes. As I try it on, stroke it, hold it up to the light, I imagine the way that it will cover my head and shoulders when the sun is blazing.

A few hours later I find myself sitting in a Palestinian service taxi. All seven passengers are heading for Bethlehem. I'm in the front seat with my handbag in my lap. The city recedes behind us and the roads grow bumpier as we drive through a fading desert landscape. High up on a mountain crest with a dazzling view, the Israel Defense Forces have set up a roadblock in a little village. The line of cars grows longer by the minute. A man with an old-fashioned brass jug walks around and sells coffee in small white plastic cups. Before long a helmeted soldier with an automatic rifle on his hip ambles our way. He looks at everyone in the car, asks for my passport and examines it. I can feel my heart pounding.

"Are you in a hurry?" he smiles.

My fellow passengers sit there quietly, motionlessly, with their papers in their hands.

"Don't look at me that way, Madame," the solider says and fixes his gaze on me.

I suddenly remember stories about cars that had been shot into at checkpoints simply because somebody had annoyed a soldier. I think about Maysoun, who had to wait for hours even though she was already in labor. I loosen my new shawl.

When they finally let us through, the driver floors the accelerator and turns up the music on the radio. Dust wafts in through the open windows and mixes with the smell of smoldering brakes. One of the women in the back seat offers us nuts out of a little brown bag. I hear my phone chirp and think that it must be a text from Nadia wondering why I'm late, but it's from the local Internet provider: *Hi, Marhaba, smell the jasmine, taste the olives. Jawwal welcomes you to Palestine.*

I get out by the Church of the Nativity in Bethlehem, cross the square and walk down the hill. The road follows the slope, passes a refugee camp that has almost merged with the town and turns towards the Separation Wall. The watchtower is right in front of me. Layer upon layer of slogans and graffiti cover the wall. A bright yellow taxi appears out of nowhere and Nadia steps out, walking in my direction with a big smile on her face, hair glistening and a handbag on her shoulder.

"How did you know that I would show up right this minute?" I burst out.

She just laughs.

We sit out on the balcony and dangle our legs over the edge.

"Whew," Nadia sighs, "Finally a chance to take my shoes off."

I met Nadia during the first Intifada in the summer of 1987. Stone throwing, demonstrations, and strikes rattled Israeli society and opened the eyes of the world to the plight of the Occupied Territories. Nadia was among the women who embodied the

Intifada and carried it on their shoulders. She attended meetings, participated in demonstrations, taught her neighbors cooking and canning methods to weather the 24-hour curfews, visited injured protesters in the hospital. She had young children at home back then, hastening through the tear-gas-filled streets of Bethlehem to nurse Wissam, her infant.

Nadia turned fifty recently and Wissam is attending Bethlehem University.

As a young woman, she lived in a stone house on the outskirts of the city, adjacent to Rachel's Tomb. A vegetable garden in the back yard boasted of a beautiful old almond tree. Evening after evening we sat under its leaves and talked. Two men in the family had recently been imprisoned without trial, and young people clashed with soldiers every day. Despite the violence, there was a feeling of hope in the air. I listened to the women talk to the clatter of the tea tray that they passed around.

"If only the IDF would pull out its tanks and troops, we could build a state of our own here."

"But how about the settlements?"

"And where is the water going to come from?"

"Not to mention our own corrupt leadership."

The sky was pink and the evening prayers from the mosque in the Aida Refugee Ramp echoed in the distance. Nadia picked up a sweet almond and cracked it open on the ground. She said that it wasn't ripe yet.

The almond tree is gone now. All that remains is a big gray stump. During the "years of peace" after the Oslo Agreement was signed and the Separation Wall was built, the family tore down the house and replaced it with a four-story building. The children would each have an apartment of their own, and the ground floor would accommodate an arcade of shops and restaurants. They borrowed a pile of money to make it happen. Their apartment on the second floor featured a modern kitchen, dishwasher, bathroom, shower and Jacuzzi. In 2002 Israeli troops invaded the West Bank. What the Palestinians often call the Apartheid Wall was built in 2003. The watchtower was erected and the family was isolated once again. The wall runs straight through Nadia and Elias's garden. The building was in Area C and the watchtower loomed only thirty yards from their new balcony. Construction stopped and the financiers pulled out. Nadia, Elias and their four teenage children found themselves living in a haunted house, a memorial to an unfulfilled dream.

We sit silently and sip the sweet juice. Later we will talk about Nadia's new career working with women in the rural areas, a project to combat domestic violence and abuse, and the illness she has been battling for almost a year. I see flickering lights where there had once been olive groves and the billowing Mediterranean landscape that I have grown so attached to. Nadia shifts her weight, raises her eyes and looks out. All she sees is the Wall.

3

God Has Called Me to Live

It is four in the morning when Natasha gets out of bed. She tip-toes into the lavatory in the corridor; the smooth paving stone is cold beneath her bare feet. Although it is midsummer, the moun-tain air is cool at this time of day. Natasha slips on her cardigan and rushes off to church. The other nuns are also on their way, some of them at a trot. The older ones walk arm in arm or lean on a slender cane. The morning prayers have already begun, recited in Old Church Slavonic. Oil lamps and wax tapers spread a dusky glow, and monotonous chants break the silence. Natasha stops at the icon of the Virgin Mary, bows and grazes the hand with her fingers. Making the sign of the cross, she walks over to her place in the pews, closes her eyes and folds her hands. Gradually the voices take on new urgency, mysteriously alternating, and the flames of the candles flicker gently. Jerusalem, the city of endless memories, hovers outside the windows, a long history of faith, hope and de-spair, of tensions that never seem to ease. But Natasha's gaze rests on the altarpiece and the Christchild, his golden halo. She sways back and forth and raises her hands in supplication.

Breakfast consists of wheat porridge with butter, tea, soft bread and thin slices of goat cheese. Natasha dips a morsel of bread in her tea, munches on it deliberately and wraps her fingers around the cup as if to warm them.

She lives in Jerusalem's Russian Orthodox Convent of the Ascension, poised like a crown jewel on the slope of the Mount of Olives. The bell tower, built in the 1870s, is a popular landmark and the nuns believe that the convent is located on the spot from which Jesus ascended to heaven forty days after his resurrection. They frequently cite the Bible: "While he was blessing them, he withdrew from them and was carried up into heaven" (Luke 24:51). The convent is surrounded by a high, stone wall. If you want to enter, you ring a bell on a green gate and a friendly caretaker opens it. The grounds accommodate a church, a chapel, rows of apartments, a hostel, a kitchen, a laundry room and a library. A fragrant garden runs along the perimeter, and an olive grove containing a cemetery stands at the far end. Forty-six nuns from a dozen countries live here under the tutelage of an abbess, whom they call *Matushka* (Mother). Their common language is Russian, but Natasha also speaks English and Arabic with the Palestinian and Jordanian nuns. She has a room of her own, with a window facing south, in one of the low stone buildings. She can see out over the city, the Walls of Jerusalem and the al-Aqsa Mosque (Temple Mount) with its gold-plated dome. The Separation Wall, which slithers like a snake across the broken landscape, is never out of sight. She has a bed, a table, a wardrobe and a few personal belongings. The chest of drawers on the east side of the room contains all of her icons and a little oil lamp that never stops burning. Natasha calls it "the beautiful corner" and frequently interrupts her prayers to gaze at the Virgin Mary, to whom she is particularly devoted.

I met Natasha on a Sunday during the First Intifada. We were both young, she already a nun and I a journalist. She had come to Bethlehem to visit her sister Nadia and have dinner with her family. I remember her as bashful, almost timid, with an inquisitive look in her eyes and the air of somebody who could burst out laughing at any moment. I thought how strange it was that two sisters could be so different in their demeanors and life choices.

Now it occurs to me that maybe they aren't so different after all and that they both live for something they truly believe in.

These days Natasha is a middle-aged woman who has led a monastic life for many years. She is still slender and agile, her gaze warm and caring. She also speaks Hebrew. As a religious person living on the Mount of Olives, she is registered in East Jerusalem, which allows her to travel in both Israel and the Occupied Territories. She is the nun who usually takes care of errands in Jerusalem and maintains contact with authorities and institutions outside the convent. Her full-length dress and black veil lend her a kind of immunity, and I can picture her making her way down Ben Yehuda Street in West Jerusalem among young Israelis and tourists in shorts. Natasha, who has chosen the life of a nun surrounded by a stone wall, has greater freedom of movement in today's Israel and Palestine than Nadia, who lives in Bethlehem on the other side of the Wall.

Natasha and I are sitting out on Nadia's balcony. It is late summer 2009. Several of the nuns have been in Bethlehem for the day and plan to pick her up this evening. I hope they can give me a ride back to Jerusalem so I'll have a chance to see my Swedish friends. We have already managed to eat, talk, drink coffee, play ping-pong and watch television. Nadia's youngest son Ramez leans towards Natasha on the sofa and listens to her soft voice.

"Are you still here?" Nadia exclaims as she bustles out with an apron in her hand. "Wouldn't you like a little tea?"

A car beeps from the street and we quickly say goodbye. Natasha and I run down the stairs and squeeze into the back seat. A pale young nun is driving while Matushka sits next to her, talking and gesticulating. As we approach the Wall and checkpoint at Al Kubba Street, I start to rummage around in my handbag for my passport, but she just waves at the soldiers, bantering with them in Russian and Hebrew, and we are on the other side in no time flat. The driver steps on the gas and we're on our way back to Jerusalem.

I'm feeling a little weary after several action-packed days with Nadia and her family. Natasha suddenly puts her hand on my shoulder and whispers that I'm welcome to spend the night at the convent. Half an hour later we walk side by side through the silent garden as the darkness wraps its arms around the city below us.

Natasha was only seven years old when she came to the convent. She lived with the nuns and went to the adjacent school. At the age of seventeen she was free to leave but decided to remain and become a nun. She started off as a postulant, advanced to novice and eventually took her lifelong vows of poverty, chastity, and obedience. At the age of twenty she was besieged by doubt and depression and fell head over heels down the stairs on one occasion. It may have been an epileptic seizure but Natasha took it as a summons: God was speaking to her in his own way. Monastic life has not been simply silence and prayer—she has also gone through crises, departures, and returns. But she has never abandoned her vows.

"I believe that God has called me to live this way," she says.

Natasha was born and raised in Beit Sahour, a Christian town near Bethlehem. She was the second youngest of six children. Her mother, a housewife, and her father, a painter, belonged to the Greek Orthodox congregation in Bethlehem. Her father died of cancer when she was six and Nadia, the oldest child, took care of her siblings while her mother worked to support the family. So Natasha and her younger sister were sent to the convent in Jerusalem.

Natasha remembers the sense of destitution that fell over their household after her father's death. She says emphatically that she has fully embraced the life she leads but cannot completely understand how a mother could voluntarily give up her children.

"It got in the way of our relationship," she says. "Every time she came to visit there was feeling of guilt in the air. She had an armful of presents and said that she loved me, but something was gnawing at her even if I couldn't put my finger on it."

The garden is redolent of soil and tall pine trees. We talk about the Russian Orthodox tradition and the life of obedience she has chosen. And why the concept of obedience is so disconcerting for me. For her, it is far from the simple question that many people seem to think. But who is to say that life should be easier at a convent than in the outside world? "What happens to someone,"

I muse, "who spends so many hours a day in contemplation and prayer?"

"It's like breathing," she says. "God, the Holy Spirit, dwells within the breath. I am an instrument, a vessel. A tiny reflection of all that is."

She offers me big, glistening cherries from a little box and we spit out the pits on the path that wends its way between the pine needles and cones.

"Don't you ever have any doubts?"

She shakes her head as though I haven't understood a thing. "Of course I do."

She takes out her key, turns on the light and makes up the guest bed in her room. I tiptoe out to the lavatory in the corridor. The floor is cold and smooth beneath my bare feet. When I return, Natasha has taken off her veil and let her long hair down. I ask her what she thinks about the Wall and everything that is happening in her country. She sits on the edge of her bed and says that things are worse than ever. It may seem calm on the surface, but the complexities, poverty, and obstacles to peace have never loomed larger. With that she lowers the flame in the oil lamp by the icons and turns off the light. I lie awake for a long time and listen to the sounds outside: dogs scampering around on tin roofs, objects falling, scraping, rustling in the wind.

When the morning prayers, recited by voices so full of pain and restrained fury, awaken me a few hours later, Natasha is already gone.

4

In the Light of God's Love

A devout seeker of truth, Jean Zaru is a widow going on seventy. She brings a chair out for me, takes off her jacket and asks if I want anything to drink. Her gaze flits above the housetops and antennas of Ramallah, shrouded in an almost compulsive silence by the August heat and calm of Ramadan—everything moves slowly, on the edge of irritation, hunger, and thirst. Is it fasting and prayer or obedience that holds this society in its grip, that murmurs its way through its streets and alleyways?

While some of the women I approach appear to have been disconcerted, Jean imparts a sense of generosity and hospitality in everything she says and does, a desire to communicate and integrate theology and politics, words and action, feelings and events.

I had shown up an hour early this Saturday morning. The Palestinian Authority had decided to eliminate daylight savings time this summer to make life easier for Muslims who fast whenever the sun is out. As a result, Israel and East Jerusalem are one hour ahead of the West Bank. So I find myself crossing not only geographic borders but time zones as a private taxi whisks me from Jaffa Gate in Jerusalem through the new tunnels towards Qalandia checkpoint—a gigantic opening in the Wall with the West

Bank that is like a cross between a maximum security prison and an international airport.

I call Jean to tell her that I am on my way and that I have just realized my mistake about the time. She is totally unruffled. "I'm looking forward to it," is all she says. "Just give me a little time to get ready."

As the taxi rolls up the hill towards her house, she clutches her cell phone in her left hand and waves to us with her right hand. We sit down in the enclosed courtyard under the shade and ambience of an olive tree.

"My first question might not be about theology exactly," I begin a little tremulously.

She plops her tray down on the table. That's all she needs to get her started.

"Are not justice and theology intimately connected? If we cannot ask about justice and equality from the perspective of the world we live in, we sacrifice all credibility as theologians—both in our own eyes and in the eyes of others. The prophets of ancient Israel proclaimed—and despaired of—justice and equality, and we are in the same position now. Justice for whom—the issue is as alive and urgent as ever.

"I have become increasingly aware that the biggest problem is not patriarchy or individual men but what I call 'structures of dominance.' We need to bring these structures to light and change them. You see them everywhere—the churches, the schools, the boardrooms, and chambers of national and international decision makers. They even find their way into liberation theology—maybe we carry them within ourselves too. Far more women than men pray, attend services and participate in community projects and activities."

Jean and her family belong to the Society of Friends (Quakers), founded by American missionaries in Ramallah back in 1886. The Quakers are known for their non-hierarchical organization, as well as their commitment to peace and nonviolence. Jean and her husband Fuad both taught at the Ramallah Friends Schools for many years. Jean is also among the founders of the Sabeel

Ecumenical Liberation Theology Centre in East Jerusalem and a former member of the Central Committee of the World Council of Churches. The outlook of women and their position in patriarchal Arabic culture are integral to her worldview.

"I like to say that women are closer to heaven. We bear and sustain it just like we shoulder the day-to-day struggle."

The battle for women's rights is closely intertwined in her mind with the goal of national liberation—with the idea and language of divinity—and she says that she always seeks to speak of God in inclusive, welcoming and gender-neutral terms.

"God is greater than our ideas of masculine and feminine, beyond our limitations. God transcends the boundaries that our religious orders and traditions have drawn. Allah and the God we believe in are one and the same. Allah is the Arabic word for God. But the question that remains is whether the God we pray to is belligerent and possessive—or loving and just. We must interpret what we read in the Bible, in the same way that we must interpret and contemplate the world we live in."

Jean returns to the tension between receptivity to God's will and trying to define it, between the prophetic call for peace and justice and the clergy's need for order and limits. And she is inspired by the prophetic denunciations of Ezekiel, Isaiah, Jeremiah, and Micah.

Ah, you who join house to house, who add field to field,
until there is room for no one but you, and you are left to
live alone in the midst of the land! (Isa 5:8)

Women's equality and Palestinian justice are also tied to the longing for restoration of a divine order that has been shattered by human conflict. Jean sees the Israeli occupation of Palestinian land as a threat to the environment, to the Creation itself.

"Water is a vital question here," she continues. "It is a matter of life and death. The military occupation and the Israeli settlements appropriate and consume huge quantities of water from Palestinian agriculture, industry, and civil society. Gaining control over water resources is part of a conscious policy aimed at colonizing East Jerusalem and the West Bank, as well as a reason for building the Wall.

"The Wall is not only a violation of international treaties and conventions but of the Creation that has been bequeathed to us."

Human beings rather than the land itself are holy in Jean's eyes, and they are responsible for its care and protection. She says that holiness can be used as a weapon and blunt instrument, but then the word loses all significance.

"We are engaged in a political battle, not a religious one. But the occupying power frequently exploits religious arguments to defend its aggressive, single-minded policies. They say that the land belongs to them. I say 'the land is the land.' It is neither holy nor promised by virtue of its mere existence. Ownership of land or soil by a people does not bring reconciliation or fulfillment of a promise. The true realization of promise and reconciliation is the emergence of peace and justice.

"A Jewish reading of Deuteronomy can arrive at the same interpretation—the covenant in the Hebrew Bible is with God. Fidelity to God, not ownership or control of land, is at the heart of the covenant."

Jean believes that the Bible has a deeper purpose than appears on the surface—to transform humanity and make it receptive to God's truth.

"God is greater than our concepts and ideas."

As she begins to speak of the soul, her voice softens and she hesitates, grasping for words.

"As the beloved ones, human beings must allow themselves to be transmuted in the light of God's love. Unless we are reconciled with ourselves, how can we be reconciled with others? My belief is that we should be sensitive and open to the spirituality of everyone who carries the light of God within them."

According to Jean, many Christians in the Middle East seek consolation in an eschatological and spiritualized reading of biblical stories. They believe that the Kingdom of Heaven about which Jesus speaks will arrive in another time and place and that the duty of a Christian until then is to watch, pray, and turn the other cheek.

A central tenet of Christian faith is the exhortation to love one's neighbor—and, with Jesus as a model, one's enemy as well.

"Palestinians are often asked that question as the shells and tear gas rain down upon us. The same day as our teenagers are arrested and beaten, the same day that water is stolen from our farmers, somebody comes up to us and asks, 'As followers of Jesus, don't you have a responsibility to love and forgive your enemies?'

"I experience that as an insult, as ignorance about the balance of power between the Israeli army and Palestinian civilians. Can you demand that an unarmed girl love an armed soldier? No, the entire assumption behind the question is unreasonable and immoral. If I truly love my enemies, I don't want them to maintain anything by means of power and violence. I don't want to see them trample on people, shout, insist on their rights from a position of dominance and control—I want them to open up and understand that this land, this creation, consists of more than acreage and square feet to be claimed by one ethnic group or another. If I love my enemies, I want them to lay down their weapons, to be human beings in my presence and in their own. Loving one's enemies never means accepting their violence and their aggression."

"As an occupied people, we have two options," Jean continues. "One option is to avoid confrontation, to collaborate with our adversaries in order to survive. That path does not lead to change, either in ourselves, our adversaries or the situation in which we find ourselves. The second option is to resist, but to do so nonviolently. As far as I am concerned, nonviolence is the only path worth taking."

How can Palestinians resist in their everyday lives? What I see is humiliating passivity and silence rather than protest or struggle.

"Our resistance," she says, "is the refusal to accept what is happening, to find the words to describe our perceptions and experiences. Jerusalem, for example, is being subjected to ethnic cleansing and that's exactly what we should call it."

Straining a little, she assures me that demonstrations and meetings are held every day. "We aren't silent. Those who fail to speak out collaborate with the oppressor and become part of the apparatus of abuse. We must break that pattern once and for all."

We drink coffee out of small cups and get up to wander around the courtyard every now and then. The sun makes its way across the vast pale sky. Jean returns a phone call and I reply to a text, moving toward the shade of the house. When we stretch out with our legs on two wobbly footstools, our eyes fall on swirls of protruding veins.

"It looks like you and I have the same problem," Jean laughs.

"Don't you wear support stockings?"

"Yes, in the wintertime. But in the summer, when I need them most, it's too hot."

5

A Household that Celebrates Life

The family album in the bookcase of Jean Zaru's brightly lit living room contains fading photographs of picnics and birthday parties. I look at the faces of her siblings, husband, children, and grandchildren. Children who are always in a hurry, who stop by for a bite to eat—but then their phones ring and off they go. Some of the pages are empty or half-empty. Jean's brother Hanna Mikhail is among the thousands of Palestinians who disappeared during the war in Lebanon and never returned.

Jean has not been in Jerusalem for many years. Palestinians living in the West Bank and Gaza have been barred from the city, and from Israel in general, ever since it was closed in 1993 and the Wall was built in 2003. A special permit by the IDF is needed in order to enter Jerusalem and gain access to its churches, hospitals, marketplaces, and public agencies. The permits are issued on a highly arbitrary basis. And the Wall is at a safe distance from the hundreds of thousands of Israelis and foreign tourists who come to Jerusalem every year. The reality of life under occupation is hidden from their view. A tourist, pilgrim, or backpacker in Jerusalem encounters a vibrant city of marketplaces, small shops, chanting and ringing church bells. Veiled women and Orthodox Jews scurry to the Wailing Wall. Alrov Mamillia Avenue, whose limestone streets and luxury shops exude an air of lavish Orientalism, have linked the walled city with the entertainment and shopping districts of West Jerusalem ever since 2008. But for those who know that Palestinians from the West Bank and Gaza cannot come here—that land and houses have been expropriated on the hill below King David's Palace, who have seen people driven from their homes, young boys arrested and interrogated—the facelift takes on a different quality altogether.

"Sometimes it feels like I'm living in Absurdistan," Jean says. "I can go to Europe or the United States anytime I want. But not to Jerusalem."

She prays, "I lift up my eyes to the hills—from where will my help come?" (Ps 121). But when she looks up to the hills around Ramallah, all she sees are Israeli settlements circling them like an ever-growing string of pearls. The locations of the neat and tidy suburbs for young families are selected for maximum geographic and military advantage. Their sprinklers are on 24 hours a day.

"They are a constant reminder of the Israeli expansion that continues unchecked while Palestinian towns are strangled and brutalized by poverty and impotence, by lack of water, land, and faith in the future."

A network of new "bypass roads" connects the settlements with communities in Israel proper. Israeli society is increasingly segregated. Not even apartheid South Africa had separate roads for its black and white citizens.

"We never run into Jews in our daily lives," Jean says. "That makes it impossible to have a respectful personal relationship with them. The only Israelis we encounter are soldiers, as well as the settlers who cite the Hebrew Bible to support their goal of gathering all Jews in 'Greater Israel.' The movement has the widespread support of fundamentalist Christians around the world, which is a big problem for us. Ironically, such Christian Zionism is pro-Israeli from a political point of view but anti-Jewish in the religious sense of the word. As Israeli policy becomes more aggressive, the settlement project encounters less resistance. For example, Western Europe exports tractors and bulldozers to Israel, while produce from the settlements is sold in virtually every European supermarket. It's true that the EU challenges and criticizes Israel every once in a while, but that has little impact on our daily lives."

Suddenly I notice that the light has shifted and there is a hint of coolness in the air. A thin veil shimmers across the sky. We go inside and I look around her living room, the embroidered cushions on the sofa, the small ornaments. Her tablecloths come from Damascus: thin, with recurring loops and patterns—one white and one orange. I have similar tablecloths back in Sweden, only one of them is blue and the other is wine colored. Hers are in better shape than mine, which have acquired stains and tiny holes through the years.

I run my hand and across one of her tablecloths, feel the smooth, slender seams.

Jean opens the refrigerator, takes out small plastic containers of various dishes that she had prepared the day before and puts them in the microwave. She talks about the sustainable, vibrant household as a real and tangible presence in the lives of most Palestinian women, about cooking with local, natural ingredients instead of buying prepared imported products.

"It's environmentally friendly, healthy and financially sustainable. And it's all part of the resistance, because it strengthens the local Palestinian economy."

Perhaps people who feel that they have gained some control over their own health and finances are better positioned to change what is going on in the world around them. The Palestinian grassroots movement often refers to the phenomenon as empowerment. Jean gives me a short but earnest lecture about the importance of buying local Palestinian lemons during the harvest, squeezing them and storing the juice as little ice cubes instead of shopping for expensive imported fruit year round.

"It's healthier, tastier, and cheaper that way. And part of the political resistance. When Jesus talks about the Kingdom of God, I think of it as a household of life in which fairness and justice are unassailable. I want the Church to be that kind of household too, a place where everyone's voice can be heard and where women and men are treated with the same respect. But we're not there yet." She shrugs her shoulders in a knowing, slightly resigned way.

Jean takes out some yogurt and cucumbers and slices the tomatoes. She serves stuffed cucumbers, eggplant, stuffed vine leaves, finely chopped lettuce and yogurt with mint and bread.

"Sharing a meal is a symbol of friendship and intimacy," she says.

Suddenly I'm at a loss for words. I'm both overwhelmed and exhausted by the search for a way to understand her and capture her tone.

All at once she strikes me as a solitary, complex being in the midst of a brutal world.

"Perhaps . . ." she muses, looking around and lighting a candle on the table, pushing the dish a little to the side.

Back in Sweden, we slice cucumbers crosswise into thin, slippery disks. But Palestinian women cut them lengthwise. I take a bite of a cucumber stick—it's juicy and crunchy between my teeth. We don't hear a single voice or car outside. Ramadan is here and all of Ramallah seems to be asleep, except for the two of us sitting at this lavish table.

"Do you want to say grace before we start eating?" she asks

We lower our heads and clasp our hands.

6

Seeking and Service

O n the way back I ask the driver to let me out in el-Azariyeh at a sharp bend in the road. I walk up a hill towards the house where Jesus' friends—the siblings Martha, Mary, and Lazarus—are said to have lived.

> Now as they went on their way, he entered a certain vil-
> lage, where a woman named Martha welcomed him into
> her home. She had a sister named Mary, who sat at the
> Lord's feet and listened to what he was saying. But Martha
> was distracted by her many tasks; so she came to him and
> asked, "Lord, do you not care that my sister has left me to
> do all the work by myself? Tell her then to help me." (Luke
> 10:38–40)

I think about the theology of everyday life and about the friendship that slowly emerged during the dinner we had shared.

Although el-Azariyeh (the biblical town of Bethany) is only three miles from Jerusalem, few tourists find their way here because it is in the West Bank. The Wall effectively cuts off the entire community and everything seems poorer and grimier for each year that passes. Children in discolored, outgrown T-shirts trail behind me with cheerful, importunate shouts.

The building is all locked up, but before long a man comes running with a key ring and a woman brings out a little table, reaching into her basket and taking out tiny brown bottles of "genuine myrrh" that she sells for ten shekels each.

The house is dim and dusty inside. The furniture is covered with faded cloths and brass vases contain plastic flowers that have lost their resilience. The custodian follows me with his gaze, never far away. He reminds me of the biblical story and I imagine Martha taking care of the dishes while Mary sits at Jesus' feet.

I go outside, walk up a little hill and down to the cave that contains the grave where Jesus is said to have raised Lazarus from the dead. The air is dark and dank—only a little gleam of light finds its way in. I feel breathless, alone, enclosed, beyond history. Is it just another musty cellar—or the abode of signs and miracles? The brightness almost blinds me when I go back outside and turn my eyes towards Jerusalem. I knew that the road on which Martha, according to the Gospel of John, went out to meet Jesus after the death of Lazarus should take us the whole way to the holy city. But it comes to an abrupt halt—cut off, almost nonexistent now. Thirty feet of military concrete loom over the grave of Lazarus.

The Wall separates el-Azariyeh and Abu Dis from Jerusalem and ensures that nobody can get to hospitals, jobs, marketplaces, or shrines.

How did that all happen? As if conjured out of thin air.

And the tale of a man whom everyone believed to be dead but rose from his grave ebbs out of my consciousness. The story of another man, who ate and drank and performed miracles in the home of Simon the leper, takes on a singular quality underneath these blocks of concrete.

I buy a bottle of myrrh on the way back and try to imagine Martha and Mary juggling chores, conversations, and meetings like modern urbanites. Two sisters imprisoned in their roles? Or was that necessarily true? I remember what Jean had just said.

"When I was a young girl, the story of Martha and Mary and the way it was used would upset me terribly. Why didn't Jesus also acknowledge Martha and what she did? I thought that faith without deeds was meaningless.

"Now I believe that the story is all about the tension between contemplation and action, something that everybody—women in particular—can experience and relate to today. The usual interpretation is that Mary, who steps outside traditional gender roles, is the virtuous sister in Jesus' eyes, whereas Martha is active, conventional, and less of a seeker. And to make things worse, she complains about her sister."

Jean ruminates about that interpretation and the way it is used to demean practical labor—so contrary to what she thinks Jesus believed. She refers to Meister Eckhart, a thirteenth century Dominican mystic, who interpreted the story quite differently and pointed out that Jesus assured Martha that Mary—even though she sat there, listened and chose to be in Jesus' hypnotic presence—would also reap her reward one day by becoming Martha's equal. Jean says that she had never read anything in commentaries on the Gospel of Luke that came anywhere near Meister Eckhart's view, and she regards that lack of insight as apprehensiveness about Christian practice—the terror of action and deeds is even greater than the fear of women's intellect.

7

At the Wall, Next to the Wall

The Wall has an opening, a border crossing between the West Bank and Jerusalem. It consists of metal screens and barbed wire, hastily built booths made out of rough planks and corrugated steel, rows of revolving doors, X-ray machines, conveyor belts and detectors. Everywhere you look are soldiers—some with helmets or luminous vests. Concrete and plastic traffic cones are moved here and there as needed. Travelers from nearby towns and villages—farmers, lawyers, homemakers, schoolchildren, and college students—wait in rickety busses, public taxis, dusty and shiny Mercedes, all subject to the same nonchalant and arbitrary justice.

The whole scene is a cross between an international airport and a recycling center. I'm sitting on the bus and flipping through my passport—I have nothing to worry about and nothing to lose. Once I get to Jerusalem, I'll walk up to my hotel, take a shower, go down to the narrow street and flop down at a cafe. I'm planning my next step after that. But still—these hours I spend at border crossings suspended between occupied and conquered territory are highly emotional. I'm seized by feelings of anger and humiliation, assaulted by questions. What happens to people who suffer these indignities several times every day? A soldier with lipstick on walks by my window—why do I notice that detail about her, or the fact that she carries her gun with such self-possession?

Thousands of Palestinians walk, drive, or ride through the crossing every day. They wait and wait, even though all of them have the required permit to commute between the West Bank and Jerusalem. Lines of vehicles wend their way along as soldiers wave them back and forth. International monitors are on site early in the morning. Wearing workaday vests with the names of various organizations, they carry notebooks, cameras, and stopwatches, count each and every passenger, document and report incidents of abuse. They serve as badly needed witnesses. But who in the international community is demanding that the Wall simply be torn down?

Palestinians wait there hour after hour. Some of them are rounded up, questioned, strip-searched. Others are left sitting on the ground. Apples, sanitary pads, scarves and notebooks roll out of their bags, later to be thrown into light blue sacks and dragged away at dawn. I once left the little silver cross that Natasha gave me in a see-through plastic case on the conveyor belt at the Abu Diis checkpoint.

"Can't you go already?" the soldiers finally yell.

Then Jesus was led up by the Spirit into the wilderness to be tempted by the devil. He fasted for forty days and forty nights, and afterwards he was famished. The tempter came and said to him, "If you are the Son of God, command these stones to become loaves of bread." But he answered, "It is written, 'One does not live by bread alone, but by every word that comes from the mouth of God.'"

Then the devil took him to the holy city and placed him on the pinnacle of the temple, saying to him, "If you are the Son of God, throw yourself down; for it is written, 'He will command his angels concerning you,' and 'On their hands they will bear you up, so that you will not dash your foot against a stone.'" Jesus said to him, "Again it is written, 'Do not put the Lord your God to the test.'"

Again, the devil took him to a very high mountain and showed him all the kingdoms of the world and their

splendor; and he said to him, "All these I will give you,
if you will fall down and worship me." Jesus said to him,
"Away with you, Satan! For it is written, 'Worship the Lord
your God, and serve only him.'" Then the devil left him,
and suddenly angels came and waited on him.
Now when Jesus heard that John had been arrested, he
withdrew to Galilee. (Matt 4:1–12)

As the battle of wits over the Hebrew Bible proceeds, Jesus gradually rejects any claims to supremacy and adopts a posture of cautious obedience to God. Instead of claiming the whole world as his domain after the devil has tempted him, he settles back down in Capernaum, where he summons his first disciples. He eschews magnificence and spirituality for that which is close at hand.

To the extent that Jesus is engaged in an inner struggle, a monologue, he appears to be winnowing out biblical passages that invest him with power and divinity in favor of those that place him in a subservient position. Everyone who reads the Bible faces the same choice. Theologian Gustaf Wingren sees the passage as a key to the gospel and the fundamental message that Jesus came to convey, arguing that he refused to live up to the expectations of a messiah.

In my mind's eye, Jesus neither lies at the foot of the Wall nor demands that it be demolished. He refuses to play the game, repudiates ideology, stresses the human factor, and shreds his opponent's arguments. And he proclaims that the Kingdom of God has come upon us.

8

God in the Belly

Marwa Nasser texts me as a reminder that the taxi is on its way and, like a solicitous parent, makes sure that I'm all right—aside from the fact that I'm an hour early once again. One of her sisters was just married and she had been visiting her parents to help with preparations for the wedding, which is a deadly serious, time-consuming, and expensive affair in the Bethlehem district. In addition to food for five hundred guests, alcohol, music, and entertainment needed to be ordered, not to mention a newly painted car to take the bride to church and a professional filmmaker to document the three-day festivities.

I can't help wondering what weddings symbolize in contemporary Palestine. Hope for the future, a statement of resistance? My sense is that the more circumscribed daily life becomes, the greater the significance that these celebrations take on. They are also an act of solidarity: each guest contributes financially, discreetly and unassumingly, so that not even the most extravagant events are a hardship on the families of the bride and groom.

Now that the wedding is over and the couple has left on their honeymoon, an air of indolence hovers over the house. It's early in the afternoon, time to rest; Marwa lays her youngest son down on the plush sofa and puts on a Disney cartoon.

"We're just going to talk a little," she tells him.

Her hair is in an updo and she has large hanging jewelry on. She is wearing a new T-shirt and a pair of harem pants that sag nonchalantly on her hips. The bright living room is elegantly furnished. A modern kitchen faces the north and a newly built veranda with a view looks eastward.

Beit Jala is an old Christian town in the immediate vicinity of Bethlehem. The medieval stone buildings in the narrow alleyways, the brooks, churches and foliage create a Mediterranean atmosphere of generosity and sobriety. The majority of the population is still Christian, and resistance to the Occupation has deep roots here. Beit Jala has lost much of its land through the years, both to settlements and the encroachments of the Wall—the size of the population and the standard of living have steadily declined. The Wall and the gigantic new settlements clash with the pale yellow landscape of olive trees, grapevines, and grazing sheep. Linked by a labyrinth of separate roads and tunnels, the settlements reign supreme on the surrounding heights. The tantalizing nearness of Jerusalem makes the residents of Beit Jala, who are prohibited from using the roads, feel even more vulnerable and isolated from their cultural and historical heritage.

The phrase "wounded memories" flashes through my mind.

Marwa was an active member of a Lutheran congregation in Bethlehem—choirs, summer camps, and pageants—even when growing up here with her three sisters. Despite her enthusiasm and devotion, she was always the one to raise questions and doubts.

"I found out at the age of fourteen that European women could be ordained. That was so incredibly cool, and I decided that's what I wanted to be."

She went on to obtain a bachelor's degree in theology at the American University of Beirut. The bishop encouraged her to follow the powerful calling that had become so much a part of her. The Lutheran congregation in Bethlehem allowed her to preach and conduct services but postponed any discussion about ordination. Even though the question had low priority among church leaders in both Jordan and Palestine, Marwa was confident and remained in school.

The bombardment of towns, villages, and refugee camps during the 1996 Israeli invasion of Lebanon disrupted her studies. It was also the period during which she met her future husband, an Austrian organ builder by the name of Christian.

Marwa is as enamored as ever of preaching and the Bible, particularly the parables and proverbs. She is deeply moved by the way that Jesus relates to others.

"How can we receive and cherish his words in our own lives?" Perhaps by approaching the people whom he met, by trying to understand what they felt and perceived. How did the encounters change and affect them?

"If the gospel of Jesus is to have any meaning for the modern world, it must engage our hearts, our bodies, and our intuition. Everyone has their own way of admitting divinity into their experience—mine is through gut feeling, a kind of sixth sense. That quality may be the most important thing we can teach our children. The process of growing up and becoming an adult seems to deprive many people of their natural receptiveness to the voice of God. My fondest desire is that I will never lose that ability and that I can pass it on to my children."

Marwa is well-versed in Palestinian theology and has adopted it as her own. Nevertheless, she has always had trouble reconciling the image of Jesus as a liberator and savior with the fact that he was a man and referred to as a king.

"Finding my place in a narrative that inevitably places men in the foreground is a constant challenge. And how can I acknowledge the Bible as a source of Jewish ethics and sensibility while my people are being oppressed and displaced by an army composed entirely of Jews?"

Naim Ateek's *Justice and Only Justice* has meant a lot to Marwa. The rage and demands for justice in the Hebrew Bible are central to his argument. As a Christian in the Middle East, she sees contextual theology not as a strand of her faith but as its very foundation.

"You can't be Christian here without taking a contextual approach. Reading the Bible literally is out of the question for me, and interpreting it eschatologically or existentially doesn't work either. That's a kind of escape, a limitation.

"The Bible itself is highly contradictory. Read Joshua or the Sermon on the Mount and you'll be struck by the conflicting messages and injunctions. I can relate to the Bible only as a path, a source of inspiration in my search for God. But there are also other wells to tap for those who find themselves on the same quest."

When Marwa realized that she was unlikely to be ordained by the Lutheran Church in Bethlehem anytime soon, her studies turned to teaching, spiritual guidance, and family counseling. She lived in Germany, followed by several years in the United States. She dabbled in yoga and meditation, experiencing a sense of transformation when she incorporated the body and physical wellbeing into her spiritual and personal development.

"I am by nature a restless person, a seeker. Suddenly my life began to take on new contours. Parts of myself that had been stowed away came to light all at one time."

Marwa has found a way of bringing her degree to bear when encountering other traditions, and she uses meditation and yoga as a means of maintaining what she describes as inner harmony. Meanwhile, she is continuing to focus on spiritual guidance and family counseling and has decided to make her home in Austria.

Marwa does not regard herself as either an emigrant or an immigrant, but rather as an Austrian with Palestinian roots.

"I refuse to be half a person," she says, her tone turning more fervent. "I don't want to be in a constant state of longing as though I had betrayed my country. I need to have a full and satisfying life where I am, and I have truly found my home, my sanctuary. We have a marvelous little house in a village by the simple name of Dorf and I love the country, the nature and the sense of order. I can leave the children's toys out on the lawn at night, and I know where to take them to get top-notch health care."

Marwa pauses and swallows, looks over at her son, who is convulsed in laughter at the twists and turns of the cartoon.

The shadows begin to fall outside her window and I need to be leaving soon. I ask her what ever happened to her dream of being a pastor and whether she had maintained contact with the bishop. I think about the resources that the church turns its back on by not ordaining women.

"Yes, we stayed in touch," Marwa answers tersely. "But they never arrived at a clear decision. I prayed to God for the opportunity to serve. Now I have chosen another path."

And we zoom off down the hill through the chaotic afternoon traffic of Beit Jala and into Bethlehem. Her son is in the back and I sit in the passenger's seat clasping the dashboard. Not an inch to spare.

"Driving is serious business here, but don't be afraid. I'm pretty good at it."

Looking at my notes later that evening, I remember Marwa leaning forward (maybe when she was talking about faith as a gut feeling) and I wonder what tradition her ideas fit into. As an aside, she had suddenly asked, "Does that make any sense?"

Two images have still not faded from my retina. Marwa at the wheel, the afternoon sunlight floating down from Beit Jala towards the Shepherds' Fields like strands of yellow hair. And children's toys strewn across a bright green lawn.

9

"The Occupation is a Sin"

It began in the dark. In 1985 a group of South African clergy published a document entitled *Kairos, South Africa*, a plea for solidarity with the anti-Apartheid struggle.[1] The signatories were anonymous, many of them in prison. In addition to articulating a theological interpretation of the situation in their country, they urged churches around the world to raise their voices against oppression.

Kairos is one of the Greek words for time, with an emphasis on the right or opportune moment. The document was widely disseminated and proved instrumental in the ultimate downfall of the Apartheid regime.

Kairos Palestine is a similar theological and ecumenical document, the first of its kind in the Middle East. Published in December 2009 and signed by sixteen religious leaders of the Eastern Orthodox, Oriental, Catholic, and Lutheran churches in Palestine and Israel, the document is subtitled "A Moment of Truth: A Word of Faith, Hope and Love from the Heart of Palestinian Suffering." Kjell Jonasson, a Swedish pastor and the West Bank coordinator of the Ecumenical Accompaniment Program in Palestine and Israel,

---

1. *Kairos South Africa*. South African History.

told me in October 2009 that *Kairos* represents the most important theological development in Palestine for many years.

The document is unabashedly contextual, proceeding from the perilous situation in Palestine: lack of self-determination, a wall that "has turned our towns and villages into prisons," barricades, blockades, expansion of illegal settlements, harassment at checkpoints, etc. *Kairos* describes the context as unsustainable and places the responsibility squarely in the lap of the Israeli Occupation. The document also examines long-term issues such as political prisoners, family reunification, the status of Jerusalem, and repeated violations of international law by the occupying power. And the Occupation is unapologetically characterized as a crime, a "sin against God and humanity" in theological terms.

The Occupation as a sin—a concept that deserves further attention.

Kairos declares:

> any theology, seemingly based on the Bible or on faith or on history, that legitimizes the occupation, is far from Christian teachings, because it calls for violence and holy war in the name of God Almighty, subordinating God to temporary human interests, and distorting the divine image in the human beings living under both political and theological injustice.[2]

Kairos criticizes support by Western churches for the theology that justifies the Occupation and corrects the history books when it comes to the creation of the State of Israel: "The West sought to make amends for what Jews had endured in the countries of Europe, but it made amends on our account and in our land. They tried to correct an injustice and the result was a new injustice."[3]

Those who drafted the document, of whom there were many more than the actual signatories, stress process, cooperation, and prayer. Rarely have so many churches collaborated so closely on a theological treatise of this kind.

2. *Kairos Palestine.* World Council of Churches.
3. Ibid.

The primary purpose of *Kairos* is not to arrive at conclusive answers but to serve as a springboard for discussion. Many people have pointed out the need for Palestinian Christians to issue such a statement as a means for their church to gain credibility in an era of faithfulness and violence.

Kairos levels a scathing critique of the peace process from a prophetic point of view.

"Religious liberty is severely restricted; the freedom of access to the holy places is denied under the pretext of security."[4] The plea revolves around hope, which is linked to the contemporary mission of the church, and love, which is associated with resistance. Nor does *Kairos* lack a message for the international community, Jewish and Muslim leaders, the Palestinian people themselves or even Israelis. The weakest link is the theological discussion, which is limited to a few brief paragraphs under the heading of "A Word of Faith." The authors write, "We, Christian Palestinians, believe, like all Christians throughout the world, that Jesus Christ came in order to fulfill the Law and the Prophets," devoting an entire section to an exposition of the concept that "our land has a universal mission."[5] These ideas have given rise to the most vehement criticism of the document, which has been accused of aligning itself with replacement theology—the belief that the Christian Church represents a fulfillment of God's "election" of Jews as the Chosen People. Particularly because this argument has been used in anti-Semitic rhetoric, it has been rejected by most denominations.

The authors of *Kairos* may have been wise to avoid a lengthy theological discussion and refrain from refuting the claims of land and hegemony advanced by Israel and political Zionism. Perhaps they knew what they were doing when they decided not to describe the situation that the Palestinian people were thrust into by the formation of the State of Israel but to be that much more insistent that peace and justice be restored on the basis of Jesus' teachings. Maybe international law and human rights provide a

4. Ibid.
5. Ibid.

firmer foundation for their plea than the fine points of theology. But would another line of reasoning also make sense?

A Bethlehem theological conference in 2011 on the theme of hermeneutics devoted surprisingly little attention to *Kairos*. Nevertheless, many of the Palestinian lecturers explicitly sought historical, textual, and archeological arguments that would lend their people, particularly Christians, some kind of fundamental right to live on biblical soil. *Kairos* may already be part of that narrative. Is that an opportunity—or a dead-end street?

10

Where My Heart Is

Yasmine Khoury belongs to a people who still speak the language of Jesus. Before moving to Jerusalem when the first Arab-Israeli war broke out, her family had emigrated from Turkey to Jerusalem in the early 1940s.

The three hundred Syrian families currently living in and around Bethlehem are members of their country's Orthodox church there.

Yasmine says that she is "Palestinian to the bone"—she is Christian, faithful, devout. She has degrees from Beer Sheva University of the Negev and has taken computer science, as well as peace and environmental studies.

Even at the tender age of twenty-five, she exudes refinement and sophistication.

"Something stirred deep down when I first read *Kairos*. I had yearned for a statement like this to come along. Every word went straight to my heart."

When she was offered the position of local coordinator for *Kairos Palestine* shortly afterwards, she felt as though God had summoned her to a worthy task. Something she could call her own.

"For me, it is incredibly important to get the word out about this document and its mission. I see it as a cry from our people, even though church leaders were the ones who articulated it. We have a dual responsibility at this point—to explain what *Kairos* has to say and to encourage discussion and reflection among congregations and community organizations.

"Every Christian here should read and think about it. These questions cut to the quick and move our souls. *Kairos* is a cry from the darkness in which we find ourselves, a plea for love, resistance and peace."

In Yasmine's eyes, reading the Bible is an eternal voyage between present, past and future. Between hope and despair. Jesus' parable that "unless a grain of wheat falls into the earth and dies, it remains just a single grain; but if it dies, it bears much fruit" (John 12:24) strikes her as a powerful description of contemporary Palestine.

A silence, a lull. Neither war nor peace. And no justice anywhere in sight.

Kairos seeks to elevate the Christian presence in Palestine and serve as the voice of a minority church in a wounded land.

"The suffering and oppression that we have experienced for all these years have left their mark on us," Yasmine says. "But we also believe in a loving, fully engaged God."

She views promotion of *Kairos* as a big popular education project that is just beginning. She tells me about courses and seminars, both in Bethlehem and elsewhere, pointing out that most of the participants are women.

"They are the most active members of our congregations—I think the pattern is the same around the world," she says as she turns off her ringing cell phone.

Yasmine says that faith in Jesus Christ offers salvation and that Palestinian Christians have a special mission of peace on the path to justice and reconciliation.

Has she seen any signs of reconciliation in the here and now?

"Little ones," she says uncertainly. "The smallest of all the seeds."

The parable of a grain of wheat, as interpreted in the light of *Kairos* and the oppressive context that gave birth to it, traces a trajectory from death to life—from darkness and waiting to hope and expectancy. The idea that something must fall to earth and die before rebirth is possible strikes many people as a fundamental metaphor of Christian doctrine, "earth" usually regarded as referring to inner, existential reality. The social, political, or religious trajectory goes from the personal to the collective sphere instead. The parable leaves little doubt in that regard: "unless a grain of wheat falls into the earth and dies, it remains just a single grain" (John 12:24).

It's break time in Yasmine's brightly lit office, located in the International Center of Bethlehem. Her job is to coordinate popular education projects about the content and significance of *Kairos*, to help incorporate its message into the consciousness of the Palestinian resistance.

How does she view her role? Her plans for the future? She says that she would like to write her master's thesis on a theological question. And she is intent on maintaining a feminist perspective.

"My church—which I dearly love—won't even allow women to preach," she smiles. Realizing that she is running out of time, Yasmine gives me Lucy Thalijeh's phone number and says that I absolutely have to talk to her, she's such a special person.

"Don't be shy about calling me if there's anything else you need."

As she straightens up her desk and calls Lucy to arrange a meeting for the next day or two, the only Aramaic words I know— *Talitha cum* from the Book of Mark—echo in my head. Jesus is on his way to see the leader of the synagogue. It is one of the most moving biblical stories about his ability to effect both healing and transformation.

> While he was still speaking, some people came from the leader's house to say, "Your daughter is dead. Why trouble the teacher any further?" But overhearing what they said, Jesus said to the leader of the synagogue, "Do not fear, only believe." He allowed no one to follow him except Peter,

James, and John, the brother of James. When they came
to the house of the leader of the synagogue, he saw a commotion, people weeping and wailing loudly. When he had
entered, he said to them, "Why do you make a commotion
and weep? The child is not dead but sleeping." And they
laughed at him. Then he put them all outside, and took the
child's father and mother and those who were with him,
and went in where the child was. He took her by the hand
and said to her, "Talitha cum," which means, "Little girl,
get up!" And immediately the girl got up and began to walk
about (she was twelve years of age). At this they were over-
come with amazement. He strictly ordered them that no
one should know this, and told them to give her something
to eat. (Mark 5:43)

11

With Biblical Wrath

She wants to meet me outside the hustle and bustle of her large household. She suggests a café on the outskirts of Bethlehem— the concise directions sound vaguely familiar as soon as I hear them. As I get out of the taxi and head towards the café, I realize that it is a brand new establishment facing the building in which Nadia lives.

A young woman is sitting in the dimly lit room with her back to the door. She is wearing a purple blouse and smoking a hoo- kah, bubbles gently rising out of the bowl. She seems to be lost in thought. I stop in the doorway, look around, hesitate.

Is it really her?

"Lucy is an activist," somebody had said. "A theologian, one of the few we have," someone else had commented. According to a third person, "She's a Palestinian through and through."

Born and raised in Beit Sahour on the West Bank and having pursued religious studies at both Birzeit and Bethlehem universi- ties, she has a master's degree in theology. In her role as activist, she has participated in the *Kairos* project, one of the few women to do so, from the very beginning. Her personal history of loss and abuse is quintessentially Palestinian.

Three members of her family were killed during the Six-Day War, and their circumstances were radically altered one night in the early 1990s. Two of her brothers were in prison when clashes between Palestinian teenagers and the IDF were an everyday occurrence in Beit Sahour. One night several soldiers entered the house, arrested her father and struck him on the head with the back of a machine gun. He died after forty days in the hospital, and Lucy's brothers were denied leave to attend his funeral.

She tells the story in a tone of restrained fury. Palestinian family sagas are unique, turbulent, primal, and existential all at once. The narratives all bear a ghastly similarity until the figures assume the proportion of archetypes: a father, a brother, a prison.

I once met Umm Jihad, whose husband—a charismatic PLO official—had been killed in an Israeli attack on Tunis in 1987. She described her sudden loss in terms of tragedy—lonely nights, silence. She stopped abruptly. She put her spoon down on the glass table and said that the bereavement of dear ones was a common experience among her people. "That doesn't make the grief any easier to endure. But I know that I'm not alone."

Lucy puffs on the hookah and drinks her sweet, thick coffee. It occurs to me that many Palestinian women (not to mention men) seem to have an insatiable need for sweets, high-fat food and tobacco. Perhaps it's a strategy for numbing the pain, for enduring the humiliation. The trend toward poorer health has accelerated over the past decade. Inhabitants of the Occupied Territories suffer from the undernourishment and malnutrition that plague developing countries, as well as the ailments associated with modernity and urbanization: diabetes, cardiovascular disease, cancer, depression and post-traumatic stress syndrome.

While Lucy's family belongs to the Catholic Church, she pays little heed to such ecclesiastical distinctions. As a practicing Christian, she is deeply committed to the *Kairos* project. Having participated since the earliest stages, she regards the ability of so many different churches to come together and agree that the Occupation is a sin in the eyes of God as a groundbreaking achievement.

I mention that *Kairos* has not received much attention outside the Middle East. Undeterred, she tells me of several international conferences that have been scheduled and of the ongoing dialog that is under way. At the same time, she leaves little doubt that the primary beneficiaries of the project are members of congregations on this side of the Wall—Christian faithful with Muslim friends and neighbors.

Lucy studied theology with the clear-eyed awareness that there was no demand for women in her profession. The Catholic Church did not ordain women and she had no desire to teach. So she concentrated on peace and human rights issues, including an understanding of the Jewish and Islamic traditions. She has also focused on human rights and feminist perspectives during her involvement in the *Kairos* project. "I sat there among all the bishops and eminences. I was the youngest, often the only woman.

"Father Jamal Khader, one of the initiators of *Kairos*, was my teacher at Bethlehem University. If my memory serves me right, he was the one who invited me to join the project. I was so honored that I really wanted to do all I could to disseminate the document. Many Christians find the message liberating, precisely because it sanctions a critique of the Occupation from a biblical point of view. And because so many different churches and traditions have found common cause."

Lucy believes that all Christian theology stems from the Bible but that the specific features of Palestinian theology proceed from the experience of oppression. "The Bible itself spares no words in advocating for the oppressed and the responsibility of others to end suffering and correct injustice. Many people do not realize that Christians still live here, and the emigration of young people is a big problem. We have to urge our sisters and brothers to stay."

She lowers her voice and leans forward. "I feel as though God has sent me a personal message—remain in Bethlehem and accomplish whatever I can. I was in the United States back in 2001. I had every reason to stay, I could have had a comfortable life. But it was as if I was beginning to lose track of myself and my roots.

"My only goal is to be politically active and serve my people.

"In Palestinian society, women run the household and men make all the decisions, whether it be in the political sphere, the church, or community affairs. But the time has come for a change. And it's happening, both among the top political echelons and at the popular level.

"I think of *Kairos* as a bridge between the political and religious realms, an opportunity to involve women more fully in the decision making process.

"Another imperative is that Christians and Muslims work side by side in the resistance effort. We go to the same schools and experience the same oppression.

"There are certain limits. Interfaith marriage is still a sensitive issue. But as long as the great majority of us are barred from going to Jerusalem, such matters are of secondary importance. I can travel to the United States any time I want, even to Europe if I go through Amman. But Jerusalem is off limits."

I ask her when she was last there.

"Six years ago. And it took me six years before that to obtain a permit."

She speaks quickly and her English is excellent. When I ask her about the impulse that sparks her theology, she says that it's the experience of oppression, as if there were no other possible answer. Meanwhile, the smoke in the café grows thicker and thicker.

She talks fervently about her involvement with a Palestinian non-governmental organization that draws its inspiration from the anti-Apartheid movement in South Africa and collaborates with grassroots efforts in Palestine and worldwide on the Boycott, Divestment and Sanctions (BDS) campaign aimed at convincing Israel to respect international law and human rights. The project, which is based on the philosophy of nonviolence, solicits the backing of people and institutions in other countries to actively oppose the Occupation. The tacit support that Israel receives from financial, athletic, and cultural institutions helps blind the world to the country's repeated violations of international law.

"This has gone on longer than any other occupation and it has got to end," Lucy says, speaking hopefully of the Russell Tribunal and other international conferences, all the young people who are engaged in the BDS campaign, and her communication with the Ship to Gaza relief project.

I have one last question. Does *Kairos* pose any risks?

After a brief hesitation, she answers reluctantly that people in other countries may regard it as overly critical of Israel and dismiss what it really has to say.

I ask whether there is any validity to such criticism.

With that, she gathers up her belongings, digs out some coins to pay for her coffee and takes off down the street.

12

Until It Hurts

A time comes when arguments fall to pieces. Dialog and communication must find a new direction. The fact that people inhabit separate worlds—maybe symbolic universes—can no longer be denied. It's as though something fundamental is collapsing—or perhaps revealing itself like never before. We drive past the Separation Wall, as well as the temporary "screens" that have been erected along the motorway. Is it a noise barrier as the Israelis maintain or a military tactic to conceal Palestinian villages while the settlements glisten brazenly in all their modernity?

In the dazzling light outside the cafe after my meeting with Lucy, I picture Jesus as a liberator and fedayeen fighter. He strolls through the hills of Galilee with a coterie of young women and men in his train. "Do not think that I have come to bring peace to the earth," he says. "I have not come to bring peace, but a sword" (Matt 10:34).

Do not even the gospels advocate military struggle when one's land is threatened? But nary a Palestinian theologian has mentioned that possibility—could it be a contemporary taboo?

My thoughts turn back to the story of the widow's mite. The brief episode in Mark 12:41–44 and Luke 21:1–4 has often been used to justify poverty. Jesus' point may not have been that the widow was blessed for giving away everything she owned. Maybe his focus was on a fundamentally unjust social order, within which the widow's gift was an expression of exploitation and despair. Perhaps the common interpretation of the story is symptomatic of a failed theology.

Maybe every story from the gospel is a road sign that points to change and transformation, not only in the conscience that motivates a lonely widow but in the unjust economic and political structures that surround her. And a frightening thought presents itself to me: despite the intrinsic radicalism of Jesus' message, the official theology that the Church espouses and cultivates has always promoted subservience, whereas liberation theology has been but an historic and theoretical parenthesis.

Lucy's words come back to me, her way of speaking and her demeanor—an undercurrent of fury that somehow evades me. I admire and am frightened by it at the same time—her manner of leaving the room and closing the door behind her.

For me she embodies the theology of rage, resistance and solidarity that rises out of oppression, the cry of those who have reached the limits of their endurance.

The footsteps descending the stairway turn out to be Nadia's. The laugh and gestures, the warmth of her presence jolt me out of my reverie. "What a delightful surprise. How about making something to eat?"

Before I know it, we are standing in the kitchen peeling potatoes. She takes off her wig, and we sit down on the sofa and chat. Afterwards we go out to the city, the kind of evening when the sky overflows with stars and the moon sways gently between the antennas and church towers. We stroll arm in arm down dark, cluttered streets. Distant voices waft their way as through a sheer fabric, children playing, a blaring television, evening prayers from the mosque in the Aida refugee camp—sporadic, melancholy epistles of woe.

"Everything seems so peaceful," I say.

"Yes, but it can all change in the wink of an eye."

We walk up the hill to the university, enter a cafe and sit down at a center table although I would prefer to be by the window. Nadia orders a glass of juice and three scoops of ice cream. I smile because she has told me about her constant struggle with her weight and resolutions to eschew caloric food.

"I have such a craving for ice cream," she explains.

We talk about recent events on the West Bank, the sense of isolation that many of its residents experience, their fears about developments in Gaza and their sadness over being a divided nation.

"They have treated the wound of my people carelessly, saying, 'Peace, peace,' when there is no peace," Nadia recites from the Hebrew Bible (Jer 6:14). The Israelis confiscate more land week by week. Not much is left on which to build a Palestinian state. The impact on the health and welfare of the women I meet and hear about is unmistakable. Many of them never see a doctor and choose to give birth at home for fear of being trapped in the labyrinth of checkpoints and roadblocks.

A young woman with a baby in a little perambulator comes up and hugs Nadia. "Long time, no see. How are you doing?"

"No complaints," Nadia says.

"You have a new hairstyle, don't you? It's beautiful. You look younger than ever."

"Thank you," Nadia smiles.

13

Women and Their Experience of God

Maysoun was expecting her first child. Come evening the contractions were more and more frequent; she gathered together her toiletries, a change of underwear and a handbag of infant clothes. She told her husband to start the car and they took off. A group of soldiers, who appeared to be unusually irate for some unknown reason, stopped them at the Nablus checkpoint.

"Where are you going, don't you know that the town is closed?"

They chuckled and continued to smoke. Maysoun shivered in the cold winter drizzle. She and her husband begged and pleaded—she needed to see a midwife right away. They assured the soldiers that they would be going straight to the hospital. Finally they were allowed to pass.

They had gone no more than fifteen yards when a volley of bullets shook the car, which rattled to a stop. Maysoun's husband slumped over the steering wheel and she saw a pool of blood on the seat. A group of soldiers ran up to the car, pulled her out and ordered her to take off her clothes, including the tampon she was wearing. She lay there on the ground while they walked back and forth screaming at each other. Realizing that her husband had been killed, she prayed that she and her child would be spared. She wept and implored the soldiers to cover her up.

The Bible contains many stories about women who find themselves in perilous circumstances. Crises and solitude are often the context in which they encounter God, hear his voice or receive the message of a divine emissary. Sarah, Abraham's wife, casts out her slave woman Hagar, who wanders in the wilderness until the angel of God appears and makes a well appear to her and her son Ishmael (Gen 16:7–13, Gen 21:14–19). Hannah, who is in despair because of her childlessness, prays to the Lord and conceives Samuel (1 Sam 1: 7–17). The Samaritan woman whom Jesus asks for a drink when she comes to draw water from a well, learns about the source of eternal life and later helps to spread the gospel (John 4): But the encounters of biblical women with God lack both a face and an idiom. Stories of men who experience God or his angels have, on the other hand, been the subject of theological, normative, and artistic analysis. Abraham is called upon to sacrifice his son; Moses receives the tablets and is commanded to liberate his enslaved people; Jesus is tried, elevated, abandoned and resurrected in a new form.

But how about Hagar, Hannah, Rizpah, Sisera's mother, Martha and all the nameless women whose cries God heeds, who find their way out of sorrow and loneliness? Where are the theological, ecclesiastical, and existential perspectives that emerge from their narratives and experiences?

Mary, Mother of Jesus has a unique position in Christian tradition, the receptacle of countless generations of women's struggles, joys and sorrows. But what happened to the Bible's female warriors, the prophetesses and visionaries, the murderers, seductresses, and harlots?

After an hour and a half, a Palestinian ambulance arrived and took Maysoun to the hospital. Her daughter Fida was born on the elevator up to the maternity ward.

A Swedish journalist by the name of Birgitta Albons got to know Maysoun, who had grown bitter and self-contained, and told the story of her life in a book published by Kvinna till Kvinna, an organization that collaborates with women in developing countries. She had trouble bonding with Fida and had a tumultuous relationship with her husband's family, who claimed her inheritance for themselves and forced her to live in a smaller apartment. She was consumed by hatred for the Israelis and the soldiers who had killed her husband, repeating over and over that she would avenge his death, that she would never forgive or be reconciled with the tragedy that had shattered her life.

Participation in a support group for women who had experienced violence, humiliation, and bereavement gave her the chance to revisit the traumatic event. The group included those whose sons or husbands had been killed or left to languish in prison, whose homes had been destroyed by the army. They met in each other's homes and eventually learned to trust each other to the point that they could laugh and cry together even when sharing their most horrifying memories.

Two years later, Maysoun exudes a sense of confidence, strength, and self-esteem. She has not forgotten but learned to go on with her life. She and Fida have left her in-laws for a place of their own. She has enrolled in An-Najah National University in Nablus.

The interactions of biblical women with God exhibit a distinct pattern. Their trials and tribulations lead to a life-changing encounter with God, his voice, an angel or Jesus. Afterwards they seek someone who can affirm and acknowledge their experience, who can help them articulate and shape a narrative. Finally they are able to change their circumstances and assume responsibility for their past.

Affirmation is the lynchpin that holds the whole process together. In the absence of affirmation, be it of horror or divinity, by another person (often a woman), their experience lacks a language and a framework, a means by which it can be processed and communicated.

The trajectory from despair to encounter, affirmation and articulation becomes a vehicle to interpret the human condition and its reflection in literature. The exhortation, or challenge, is to formulate a theology and philosophy of validation, to create venues where both agony and ecstasy can find expression—a space in which God patiently awaits his creation.

Maysoun's life in occupied Palestine also traces a journey through the gospel: faith that even the most doomed and guilt-ridden of human beings can be redeemed and liberated. This dynamic and the stories it spawns must be corroborated and retold over and over without obscuring any of the pain and humiliation that Maysoun and others have suffered. The eyes and ears of others, not only women who have endured the same fate, must be opened if there is to be any hope of putting an end to the violence that is endemic at checkpoints, in the occupied territories and at the heart of the Palestinian-Israeli conflict.

The occupation begets brutality and rage; it is a sin in theological terms, a crime under international law and abuse by all human standards. Maysoun and her husband are among the victims whose story has been recorded and told. The gospel is an ongoing history, an encounter that leads from memory to hope.

14

To the Tune
of Sorrow and Exhaustion

I was on my way to buy some fish. It was my daughter's eighteenth birthday and we were going to celebrate at Signe and Ali's house in Abu Dis. On the bus to Shufat, which has one of the few seafood shops on the West Bank, I realized how close I was to the Sabeel, Ecumenical Liberation Theology Center on the outskirts of Jerusalem. That's where I met her, in the midst of a conversation with Naim Ateek, who was presenting a refreshing interpretation of the Book of Jonas. Every once in a while, a sixty-year-old woman sitting across from me made a thoughtful comment or objected to something Naim had said. In addition to being both knowledgeable and articulate, she fearlessly challenged his opinions. I made a mental note of her name: Cedar, a lofty old tree I thought as I walked up to her, introduced myself and asked her where she had come from.

"I'm from here," she gestured indignantly.

I sent her an e-mail after returning to Sweden. It took a while for her to reply. I told her about my project of writing about Palestinian theology as formulated by women and said that I would like to get together with her. She said that she had a busy schedule but that I was welcome to call any time I was in Jerusalem.

The first thing I do on my next trip is to get hold of her and suggest a date. She says brusquely that she can't make it that day, but gives me a specific time to call back. This time she informs me that her niece has just passed away.

"I'm sorry," she says, "I can't do it right now."

I wait a few days and try again although I'm starting to feel a little pushy. After a long silence, she says softly, "I apologize for putting you off, Anne, but you would do better to talk with somebody else. There are a lot of younger women who have much more to say. I'm weary to the bone and feel completely empty inside."

As we talk, I look out over Jerusalem from my vantage point. The street is bustling with merchants, camels, tourists bearing tiny cameras and luminescent caps. Cedar relents a little, saying that I can e-mail her a few questions and she will try to find time to answer them: "But I can't promise anything." My gaze still fixed on the city, I shudder and wrap my purple scarf a little tighter around my shoulders.

I e-mail Cedar in November and ask her whether she might have time to answer a few questions. I remind her that we had talked over the summer. She answers courteously and seems to appreciate my persistence. She writes again a few months later: "Anne, I need to apologize once more but I don't have very much time at my disposal and, to be honest, I'm probably a bit lazy as well. But please don't let that stop you from finishing your book."

I spend the winter writing as the wind sweeps gusts of snow off my roof. Reading Wingren, I am struck by the similarities between his creation theology and the Palestinian perspective. I take out the scarf I bought in Jerusalem and wind it around my neck. Despite its pleasing hue and fabric, it is a tad too thin for the Scandinavian cold.

15

From Exodus to Liberation

"In your steadfast love you led the people whom you redeemed; you guided them by your strength to your holy abode" (Exod 15:13).

As I was leaving, Jean Zaru leaned forward and asked, "Don't Swedish churches still use the story of Exodus as an allegory of escape from captivity? Surely they do."

"Yes and no," I answered evasively. "It's a bit of problem, of course, from a Palestinian point of view . . ."

"A definite problem," Jean said sternly.

I later regretted that I hadn't asked her why. Is it because the focus of the narrative is on the travails of a particular people, the Israelites? No, that is true of any liberation struggle. Is it due to the way that the story has been used in the Jewish and Christian traditions? No, it has also served as an inspiration to other movements for freedom and dignity. Liberation theology and gospel music constantly refer to the Exodus as a central metaphor for the ultimate triumph of the oppressed. My sense is that the basic source of the problem is that Zionist rhetoric has exploited the story, like other incidents from the Bible, as an argument for the right of the modern state of Israel to appropriate land, to expand, to deny and humiliate the Palestinian people and to erase their history.

I never asked the question because I thought I knew the answer. The biblical promise of a blooming homeland has been subverted by the claims of an oppressive state. Because the story of one people's liberation has been used to justify the subjection or annihilation of another people, Palestinians cannot see the universal message that lies at its heart. Images of escape from captivity paradoxically awake memories of their own dispossession. The ravages of political and ideological Zionism have crippled attempts to interpret the Hebrew Bible in a more ecumenical, metaphoric and timeless manner. The historical context in which the Bible has been read demeans and invalidates a God whose covenant with one people represents his love for all of humanity. The striving for liberation and self-realization at the core of the Hebrew Bible is distorted, rendered inoperative and stripped of its essence, only to be replaced by the symbolism of violence and abasement.

A kind of negative, or reified, contextualization emerges. Given the political developments of the past century, the Exodus and other biblical stories about promises and homecoming may have lost their ability to nurture and affirm the aspirations of contemporary Palestinians. Maybe, just maybe, I am wrong. But even a contemplative interpreter of the Bible like Jean seems to have reached the point at which the very story has morphed into the nefarious purpose for which it has been abused.

The Exodus from Egypt—which could represent the liberation from any captivity—and God's covenant with Abraham—which could be a promise to all refugees—no longer serves as a tale of freedom and return, so deeply ingrained in the Palestinian soul, but as a reminder of the political ideology that erects walls, carves out bypass roads, expropriates sources of water and sustenance, chops down olive trees, seizes and occupies the land of another people.

> The Lord is my shepherd, I shall not want. He makes me lie
> down in green pastures. (Ps 23)

Jean recites the psalm, and I join her. But now the green pastures are littered with barbed wire and the graves of innocents.

16

Is Faith Possible?

During a typical week in March 2012, the Israeli Committee Against House Demolitions reported that nine homes and six stables had been destroyed while fifty-two people had been displaced in the villages of An-Nazla al-Wusta and al-Jiftlik. On March 13, five homes and six stables were destroyed and thirty people (including twenty children) were displaced in Faysal al-Wusta.

This was the third time during the month that the villages, which are wedged between the Tamer and Yafit settlements, had been the victim of such attempts to expropriate their land for expansionist purposes.

I don't know why these little sheds affect me so much. How can one of the best-equipped armies in the world bring themselves to use tractors and bulldozers against the livestock of poor farmers?

Can contemporary Palestinian theology serve as a rebuttal to Zionist ideology and practice? Initially I wanted the question to remain open. But I see it increasingly as an issue that eludes the best of minds, one that has assumed enormous proportions at the same time as the answer recedes from sight.

There is no venue for the conversation, no category that encompasses such a confrontation. Theology is a product of the soul that manifests in worship and social attitudes, whereas occupation is a projection of military might.

I tell a friend of my mother that I am writing about Palestinian theology. A quizzical look appears on her face, "How could it be any different from our theology? Don't they worship the same God, read the same gospel?"

One of the last times Jesus comes to Bethany, Mary says, "Lord, if you had been here, my brother would not have died" (John 11:32).

An accusation smolders beneath her words: "Perhaps we would have been spared all our suffering if you had been with us."

Sometimes I think that the homesickness, the longing for a homeland in the Bible, is really a desire to approach and be with God. If so, the lack or loss of a homeland is a reminder of God's absence or unattainability.

The contemporary equivalent of Mary's lament might be, "If God had been here, all this never would have happened."

Is it possible to believe in a righteous, loving and caring God in a time of violence and deprivation?

In the face of Mary's recriminations, Jesus performed one of his final miracles, awakening Lazarus, who had been dead for four days, long enough for a stench to arise.

> He cried with a loud voice, "Lazarus, come out!" The dead man came out, his hands and feet bound with strips of cloth, and his face wrapped in a cloth. Jesus said to them, "Unbind him, and let him go." (John 11:44)

But is that kind of faith still possible?

17

Toward a Postmodern Palestinian Theology

Sisera, a weary Canaanite warrior who has valiantly battled the tribes of Israel, is enticed by Yael, who ignominiously kills him with a mallet and tent peg.

> Out of the window she peered, the mother of Sisera gazed through the lattice: "Why is his chariot so long in coming? Why tarry the hoofbeats of his chariots?" Her wisest ladies make answer, indeed, she answers the question herself. "Are they not finding and dividing the spoil? A girl or two for every man; spoil of dyed stuffs for Sisera, spoil of dyed stuffs embroidered, two pieces of dyed work embroidered for my neck as spoil?" (Judg 5: 28–30)

The women realize that their sisters have been the victims of violence and abduction in the aftermath of war. Their knowledge binds them together in a kind of tacit solidarity—perhaps a protest, an objection and a show of resistance.

The plight of Sisera's mother both embodies and critiques the ruthless logic of war.

The contemporary reader can choose to either hear or dismiss her testimony.

Similarly, "Rizpah the daughter of Aiah took sackcloth, and spread it on a rock for herself, from the beginning of harvest until rain fell on them from the heavens" (2 Sam 21:10) to mourn the death of her sons.

The reader can also ignore or repudiate her, but I see her as a witness who manifests despair, madness and rage. Perhaps she is suffering from post-traumatic stress syndrome or is simply reacting in a natural way to sorrow and loss.

Or is she an historical literary figure who symbolizes fury and opposition to the brutality and bloodthirstiness of men and power, the waste and corruption of human potential that has lived down through the ages?

I wonder whether Palestinian theology can open the door to an alternative reading of the Bible that places other individuals, peoples, groups, scenes and stories at center stage. Such an approach could inspire others to give a second look at biblical figures who are often sidelined but who cry out to be heard. I think about Hagar and her unique encounter with God, her trajectory from victimhood to action as inspiration for other servants, regardless of race or ethnicity.

A Palestinian reading of the Bible could entail a quest for other figures, images, fissures, inflections and sources of light between various narratives and levels of understanding, rather than a deliberate, unequivocal truth.

Can an historical interpretation of the Scriptures point the way to the future? Must they always be seen as the journey of one particular people to the discovery and knowledge of God? At what point does the contemporary reader have to reject the portrayal of a God who ignores the fate of all peoples but his own, whose proclamations are exploited to present the State of Israel as a fulfillment of the covenant. The entire New Testament can be read as a rebuttal of an exclusivist interpretation of the Hebrew Bible and its God.

But is not Jesus also a voice for the liberation of the Israelites that St. Paul broadens to encompass the heathens as well? Finding support in the New Testament for the thesis that he articulated a universal ethic is no easy task and may require a leap of faith.

Perhaps a Palestinian reading of the Bible requires an active choice of the Canaanite perspective, a focus on ethics rather than ethnicity—a narrative that arises out of the situation of women, children, and the downtrodden.

The experience of Palestinians demands the ability to forge a new sense of hope and meaning, a reinterpretation of their own circumstances that can make an important contribution to a theologically parched world, to the ongoing political and cultural battle to reconstruct a country after decades of displacement, oppression, occupation, and dependency.

Can Palestinian theology expand, unlock, and liberate the gospel outside the Middle East as well? Is it able to elicit contemplation, reflection and a bottom-up vantage point from which to observe biblical stories and images? Can it illuminate the difference between standing on the periphery of the Promised Land and actually being there, the tension between hope and fulfillment?

Or does Palestinian, contextual, and biblical theology have everything to gain—whether in the churches or at the universities—by consistently promoting the gospel of love? As Jesus taught, "In everything do to others as you would have them do to you" (Matt 7:12). These are questions I want to address in my next conversation.

18

Unexpected Rain

Nora Carmi was the moderator, and one of the few Palestinian women, at the international theological conference in Bethlehem in August 2011. She exudes the dignity of a mature woman. We sit down on her balcony with a bowl of fruit and two glasses of ice water.

Conflict has been a constant companion in Nora's life. She was born in West Jerusalem and her family fled to Lebanon when the State of Israel was founded in 1948. They returned to Jerusalem in the 1950s; her father was a pharmacist at Augusta Victoria Hospital on the Mount of Olives. He was a survivor of the Armenian Genocide at the hands of Turkey in 1915. Having lost many of his relatives, he saw himself as a member of the diaspora until the day of his death.

"I've led a blessed life," she says. "I grew up in the Old City and went to a Catholic school for girls. An Armenian priest came to visit every Sunday. I dearly loved the mysticism of the Orthodox tradition."

Nora majored in sociology at the American University of Beirut, came back to Palestine, got married and has since lived in a predominantly Muslim neighborhood—which she counts as one of her blessings.

"I have always had Muslim friends and neighbors. Our doors were never locked. I couldn't escape a sense of envy at the regularity with which they prayed—stopping everything five times a day; it was awe-inspiring.

"Faith is at the core of my relationship with God. And holiness is a vertical connection with the divinity that dwells within each of us."

Alongside of a long career as an English teacher, Nora has been deeply involved in social, human rights, peace, and ecumenical issues. She worked for the YMCA as a young teacher and has collaborated on a number of occasions with the World Council of Churches, helping to arrange World Day of Prayer. Women are the source of her strength, the magnet for her most profound commitment.

She and Anglican priest Naim Ateek built the Sabeel, Ecumenical Liberation Theology Center on the outskirts of Jerusalem. They organized summer camps at which they attempted to dismantle barriers and established patterns between the sexes and among various religious and ecclesiastical traditions.

"Simple things like asking boys to set the table. Our culture has so many layers of inequality that we need to break through."

Nora describes her life as an exhilarating journey of faith that is long from over. As a retiree, she continues to explore the promise of peace.

"My goal is to follow Jesus and promote respect and amity among all people." She stresses that such aspirations are not the exclusive purview of those who call themselves Christians.

Nora's condemnation of the Occupation is more unyielding than that of any other Palestinian woman I have met. She says that not even the Palestinians understand its extent and cynicism, that options for building a viable state on the small area of remaining land are rapidly dwindling. She is inspired by Jewish thinkers—all equally critical—like Mark Braverman, Israel Shahak, and Marc Ellis.

Ironically she also stresses the importance of forgiveness and the need to see the Other. A prolific writer, Nora published an article in 2012 about the rainstorm that caught Jerusalem by surprise on Good Friday. Pilgrims and religious tourists were wandering down the Calvary path that had been set up in the narrow streets of East Jerusalem. Some of them looked up in astonishment, perhaps remembering the biblical verse, "For he makes his sun rise on the evil and on the good, and sends rain on the righteous and on the unrighteous" (Matt 5:45). Meanwhile, the jaded locals repeated the old saw that it always rains on Good Friday. Nora thought about the humiliation of the Son of God, the ultimate sacrifice for the salvation of humanity. Her understanding of the word peace arose out of her religious faith, but it had taken time for her to realize that Jesus—who had given us the commandment to love each other—also urged us to make peace during the last week of his life. He wept over Jerusalem and said, "If you, even you, had only recognized on this day the things that make for peace! But now they are hidden from your eyes" (Luke 19:42). His very last words on the cross were, "Father, forgive them; for they do not know what they are doing" (Luke 23:34).

Nora explains her idea that forgiveness between the two peoples who live in the Holy Land requires seeing past the stereotypes they have developed of each other, recognizing divinity in each person by respecting difference and—perhaps the biggest challenge of all—acknowledging their own errors and crimes.

Jesus constantly demanded that his followers dwell in and promote peace. But none of it is possible without forgiveness.

Perhaps, I muse, forgiveness must be sought in one's own community as well.

Nora nods, "We must be reconciled with ourselves. Until that happens, we can't find reconciliation with others."

She has seen an extraordinary amount of political energy consumed in resistance to the Occupation. "But the responsibility for Palestinian society and our own relationships is nobody's but our own."

Lovely acacias with smooth white bark tower above us. Nora takes out a little plastic bottle and asks me whether I would like to wash my hands. It's Ramadan and hot outside. But the heat is easy to bear this summer. Maybe it's the altitude we find ourselves at—and the soothing breeze.

19

Like the Incense that Rises from the Mount of Olives

My thoughts coalesce around a few main themes that emerged from my encounters with Palestinian women.

Thinking of Jean reminds me of faith in care and solicitude, the desire to build a Kingdom of God in the image of a household, and of the meaning of presence.

Her daily life is interwoven in an ethic of friendship, hospitality, and devotion that constantly seeks the light of God in the other. I look back at the amity that slowly emerged during the meal we shared. She had once invited the Israeli commander-in-chief to have coffee with her and brought out her most elegant china but then took the opportunity to tell him the unvarnished truth.

She represents a realization of Jesus' ministry within an ethic of devotion.

Memories of Marwa bring me back to a theology of the body and a universal spirituality. East and West, dream and reality, shake hands in her presence.

She represents a postmodern Palestinian spirituality that proceeds from the physical and corporeal.

Yasmine symbolizes a theology of hope, action and community.

Lucy revives the ethic of resistance and I hear prophetic judgment echo in her soul. Hers is a theology of pathos, rage, and a cry for justice.

My encounter with Cedar made me aware of the need to approach sorrow and expectancy from both a biblical and contextual perspective. She may incarnate the most distinct feminist tendency of all—the search for a home that has long since been abandoned. Hers is an ethic of grief, waiting, and patience that, perhaps unconsciously, can stretch out a hand to the absurd imagery of Revelation.

In Nora I hear the voice of peace and acceptance, the theology of mature reconciliation. I sense the painstaking practice of dialogue and forgiveness based on profound knowledge of both her own people and the Other—a mission and a journey. Hers is the theology of communication, accord, and rapprochement.

My last encounter with Nadia encompasses everything that she represents for me: motherhood, presence, solicitude, and solidarity—a contextual theology of incarnation by which Jesus is a fellow human being who sees and comforts the sick and oppressed.

Thinking about Natasha evokes images of prayer as timeless space, the language of life and the call of God. My thoughts also go inevitably to the renunciation of personal property and to the fate of somebody who lives that way. Her theology embraces an orthodox belief in spiritual beings and phenomena, an expression of the presence of the Holy Ghost in someone's life when her personal space narrows. Perhaps it is a doctrine that whispers like the incense that rises from the Mount of Olives—we are neither chosen nor rejected, neither settlers nor nomads: we are all guests and strangers at a table that somebody else has set.

20

Friendship in a Time of Illness

I wake up one morning to an e-mail from Nadia.

I must tell you that after having counseled children with the disease for so many years, my time has also come. I discovered a lump in my right breast when I was teaching the women in Wadi Fukin, a nearby village that you visited with me ages ago, about the importance of regularly examining their own.

I didn't know whether to laugh or cry, but that's the way it was. I didn't say anything but went home and checked once more. And there was no way of denying what I found.

I was given a definitive diagnosis by the doctor a few days later. I kept it completely to myself. It was as though I had to digest and understand it first. And I wondered how Elias would take it, if he could cope with a bombshell like this. Finally, I sat down with the entire family and broke the news.

Now I realize how lucky I've been. I had a terrific doctor at Augusta Victoria Hospital. We went to Jerusalem without the proper papers—Natasha helped me, it's a long story. She sat at my bedside every day after the operation, watching over me and holding my hand.

I have been praying to God the whole while, especially when the treatment was most arduous. The experience has

strengthened me in untold ways. I often feel lonely and ex-
posed, yet surrounded by the kindness and love of family,
friends and co-workers.

I walk around in the sun with Nadia's words echoing in my head.

Wingren cites St. Irenaeus, Bishop of Lyons, Father of the Church, and his characterization of Jesus as a physician, a facilitator of the healing process. It occurs to me that Luther and many other medieval thinkers adopted an almost legalistic view of Jesus in which salvation is a matter of human action, right and wrong, virtue and sin. The classical doctrine of atonement relates to human beings as creatures bound by specific laws—as if the space in which we encounter God is a courtroom where we are either convicted or acquitted and generally pardoned.

But what if we are needy patients and salvation represents a return to health? What role does faith play in that process? How does our relationship with God change? Does prayer take on a new significance? Is salvation still the restoration of joy, the desire to live?

Perhaps Palestinian land and aspirations can be viewed theologically as a kind of living tissue that requires love, nourishment and rest, one that longs for healing and harmony. Certainly Palestine needs to cultivate and reclaim its harmony and beauty. The Palestinian landscape has been extraordinarily brutalized and defaced by war, poverty, barriers, conflicts, roads, settlements, military posts, disasters and prohibitions, by the contrast between the ramshackle villages and refugee camps and the shimmering settlements on the hills. Every garbage dump, field of desiccated crops or chopped down olive trees, artificially fertilized garden in the settlements, deep well, parched river bed, bank, wall, fence and checkpoint—this far-flung system of military oppression—is a reminder that the Occupation has crushed not only hope and the prospects for leading an ordinary life, but the land, soil, and environment, their natural beauty.

I flash on the time several years ago that my daughter and I visited a hospital in Jerusalem. Nadia was doing volunteer work for an organization that supported families of children with cancer. We met a five-year-old patient who was wearing a blue bonnet and cried the whole time because she had lost her hair and didn't want her siblings and cousins to see her that way.

Nadia sat at the edge of her bed for a long time and talked to her, stroking her arm.

Now I am at her bedside at August Victoria Hospital on the slope of the Mount of Olives. Natasha sits next to Nadia with her black veil turned back from her forehead, revealing her graying hair. She reads a little from a book, talks about her life at the convent. Then she falls silent and simply keeps her sister company.

A few days later, we sit out on the balcony. Tomorrow I will be returning to Sweden. It strikes me that it all began with a scarf and is ending with a wig—a kind of journey of its own.

Elias comes out with a tray of tea and bowl of nuts, plus a glass of beer for himself. He asks whether I'm thirsty, then pours half his glass into mine. The washing machine spins, shakes and beeps in its corner of the wide balcony while the neighbor's dishwasher rattles away. Otherwise it is dark and silent, white lamps glowing demurely on the wall.

"Elias was really shaken up when we received my diagnosis," Nadia says. "He cut himself off—sometimes I think he was more frightened than I was. The mere thought that he could ever lose me came as a big shock to him.

"I'm the only Christian at my job in Ramallah. Their prayers and caring make me feel peaceful and secure. They have let me start working again at my own pace, and they have been wonderfully understanding the whole time."

Tiny hairs, almost white, are beginning to appear on the top of her head. Her face is chiseled in the night air, younger and more vulnerable than before. Elias lights a cigarette and Nadia asks him something in Arabic. He glances at the clock, goes to get a plastic bag and leaves.

"It has to be washed," Nadia says.

"What are you talking about?"

"My wig."

How dumb of me! Of course, it needs to be maintained and coiffed just like the real thing.

She tells me about her hairdresser. "When he found out that I was sick and would lose my hair, he said, 'Nadia, I'm going to order a wig for you, and as long as you need it, I'm going to take care of it every week. See it as a present from me to you.'"

Elias drives up the hill towards Bethlehem turns right and parks on a side street. He enters a courtyard and knocks on the door of a hairdresser's; the lights are still on and the place is redolent of chemicals and perfume.

He gets up early the next morning. I hear the car start and the garage door close.

Nadia and I have breakfast—bread, tea, hummus, and jam. Cucumbers like little coins and a bowl of za'atar herbs. Dark green olive oil slithers over them like a glistening snake.

The light slants through the kitchen—even the Wall, the only object we can see outside the window, is beautiful this morning with its multicolored graffiti, its slogans, the will to resist etched in a gigantic concrete block.

Elias comes back and Nadia puts her cup aside, gingerly lifting the wig out of the bag and holding it up to the light. It smells clean and fresh, a touch of purple in a sea of black, shimmering, scrupulously rolled up on soft, pale blue curlers.

Bibliography

Kairos Palestine. World Council of Churches. December 11, 2009. Online: http://www.oikoumene.org/en/resources/documents/other-ecumenical-bodies/kairos-palestine-document.

Kairos South Africa. South African History. June 21, 1985. Online: http://www.sahistory.org.za/archive/challenge-church-theological-comment-political-crisis-south-africa-kairos-document-1985.

www.ingramcontent.com/pod-product-compliance
Lightning Source LLC
Chambersburg PA
CBHW071106090426
42737CB00013B/2509